Verses: 1928-1972

VERSES
1928 - 1972

JASPER ROOTHAM

RAMPANT LIONS PRESS · CAMBRIDGE

© Jasper Rootham 1972

Printed and made in Great Britain

For Joan

Author's Note

These verses are a selection from those I have written during
the last forty-four years. They are not printed in chronological
order but except for *Sibelius*, which was written in 1945, are
in general sequence with the events or poetical experiences to
which they refer. There is one exception to this. *Stalin* (page
33) was written in 1950. He died in 1953.

Some of the pieces have already appeared elsewhere and I
am accordingly grateful to the Editors of the publications in
question for having given them a first showing.

J. R.

Contents

Sibelius

The black pines, a grey lake, the sky
   Withdrawn, silent; not a sound
In all the world. A man could die
   Lying upon the cone-spread ground
Watching the lake, the sky, the pines;
   Die in the silence, mad, alone,
     Watching the lines
       Of pines
   Stretch to the cold dumb moon.

And then, across the frozen air
    Carelessly riding
  Oars a great Swan. He anchors there
   Beside the shore, and gliding
Stately upon the shattered mere,
    Sings.

He sings to break all hearts but his.
   He tells of things
Unthought till now, and purposes
   Unknown. His is the voice
Of all the Silences that ever were
   Or shall be; and the noise
Of Solitude only his ears can bear.

   At length from that secret throat
   The last and loveliest note
    of pain
   Falls and is lost. The wings
    Are spread;
    The springs
   Of song are dried, and once again
    Silence is dead.

First Love

Corn coloured, as I remember, your hair
    and admirably spun.
I used to watch it; and your forearm, where
    in the slanting sun
the down showed coppery, foreshadowing joy.
    You were breakable I used to think,
to be watched only, not touched even.
    And so when you smashed my favourite toy
in a temper, I cried.
    You were the boy
although your thighs were softer and you wore a frock
    and I,
muscular, solid, who could have broken you like a rifle stock
    upon a rock,
    was tied
    by tenderness, became a girl
and weeping learned the first lesson in the book of love.

    To India they said you went,
    to the rat-a-tat-tat
    of the Khyber pass
whither the Colonel your father had been sent
    (enormous, gallant, terrifying, kind)
    to soldier in his tent,
leading the troops to die in the wet, bitter dawn
    to die with the foe, hidden in the clefts above.

    Face it; as I lay upon the grass
    caressing the cat
it was of your father that I thought,
    not you;
    the childish mind
reverted to the pictures in the history book.

    A hundred redcoats toiling up
the brown slope bare of bushes, heather, corn
    and there aloft, waiting

the Tribesmen's boulders
levered against the shoulders
ready to fall
at a shrill signal call.
And then the death, the blood
the screaming cup
of suffering and the last incredulous look
into the glass of eternity
spattered with guts and mud.

One broken toy
a dead Colonel and an orphaned girl.
In the cruel ear of the imagination
the little I,
the eight and a half years' boy
could hear the skirl
of the funeral Gurkha pipes, the lament,
ascending into the Himalayan blue;
and my tears were not for you
but for him,
cradled for ever in his stony bed.
So the first journey upon which I was sent
by Aphrodite
ended
in love for the dead.

Second Love

It was never on.
You were eighteen a débutante and stout;
  I was thirteen and thin.
But Oh! the love that I poured
  down into your ample bust
  as you leaned out,
nightie afloat, from your window at the Boot
Hotel in Eskdale, and I, dazed as a coot,
    scored
a bullseye with a cunningly tossed pebble.
  I have never adored
    a pebble more.
It was molten with sin,
  that pebble, as it went in
through the sweet warm door
and you screeched. I thought it must
lead to something. I had, after all, scored.
  What I didn't know
was that you were put upon and bored
  but were too kind to tell me so.

4

Curlews

Why do the curlews out on the fell
Cry so loud ? The Devil can tell.
Far in the night, when the fairies play –
No man sees them, but so men say –
The Devil comes riding a flame eyed horse
With his hounds of hell and a hare at course.
The hare is a man that was damned on earth,
And his soul must serve the Devil for mirth.
Swifter than mortal hunt could be,
Over the Coolin, down to the sea,
Follow the hell hounds nose to the ground;
And the Devil he laughs with never a sound
To mortal ears – but the hare can hear
As it limps along by the silver mere.
Suddenly Mother earth shivers and gapes,
And opens while mystic changing shapes
Of smoke and flame arise; and the hare
With a pitiful dreadful look of despair,
Leaps down to Hell with the Devil and all
To be damned for ever, and no recall.
What saw the curlews out on the fell
That they cry so loud ? The Devil can tell.

Hereward Dead

Sad wind harping and sighing in the willows,
  Why do you moan so low
Over the fen, in the mist that billows
  In curves on the earth ?
There are sad sounds the world over,
  But none I know so sad
As the sob of the loveless lover
  And the crying of the wind.
Hereward is the wind's sorrow,
  The wicked and the brave,
Who never cared for tomorrow.
  And now he has no grave.
But he lies out alone with his soul fled away,
  Alone with the bittern and the reeds,
And who is to find him ? Who shall say
  Where the Wake is gone ?
Sigh on poor wind, have your fill of sighing,
  You never shall hear him again.
Hereward whom you loved, sad, dead, he is lying
  Alone with the dusk and the fen.

Grey London Houses

The garden lies, as a dull no man's land
Between the gaping houses. Overhead
Hangs smutty sky. On earth, a stealthy band
Of grass licks slily the black flower bed.

God! Send me back to the mountains
Up through the mist and the rain,
Alone by high green fountains
To drink, and live again.

The air is clear upon the hills,
No smoke of man appals:
The lavish sun in plenty spills
His honey. Beauty calls.

Why do the dull grey houses gape, and why
Does the grass lie gasping, parched like Semitic sand?
Patience, o faithless, look not with the eye,
But with the sharpened soul, and understand.

Let the grey houses gape, they are the crust
That beauty lives in. For man beauty is
And life's full essence, even be he thrust
Where dirty, sultry sky encompasses.

Love is behind the dark glass of that house,
And charity, and the beloved smile of eyes
Shining like fountains, strong as the hills to rouse
A lovely pain of happiness and surmise.

Shine bravely, sun, upon the peaks of the soul,
Dear flowers to the heart's flood lift your heads:
Love is about you, you can drink its beauty:
You took houses, let your grey windows laugh.

To H, a Friend of Long Standing

When for long months we have not seen one another,
   And circumstance brings us again
To meet, with few words and a handshake, then,
                       my mind's brother,
   Comes gentle joy. For this is no pain
Tearing at the heart, like a long-waited meeting
   of lovers: there are no words of gladness
Seeking to cover doubt. It is a quiet greeting
   Happy and sure, remote from any sadness.

We will sit talking, perhaps, of things of everyday,
   And perhaps of those that are beyond,
Seekings and doubts and failings. But we will never say
   "Try this, try that, for the sake of one that is fond
Of his friend;' There are no shackles of obligation
   To make our friendship lame:
The duties we have to each other, come as a revelation
   From within, and we give them no name.

A Lament for all Young Nuns

See the grey line of the dim religious sisters.
   They pace slowly, slowly,
   In contemplation lowly.
See, their eyes seek the ground;
   Not, O Almighty God
   Thy cloud-flecked sky
   Beckoning from on high,
Neither Thy flowers' message sweet
Nor Thy stars, which faintly greet
From the far side of Thine Eternity
The aspiring eyes of our humanity.
See the grey line of the dim religious sisters.
   See, they have been torn
     From the sin
   Into which they were born.
They will not know the cool touch of running streams
   Upon their pale limbs,
   Except in dreams:
They will not feel the rough kiss of the gale
   Where it skims,
Trailing on the moors its tattered cloak of hail,
   While they sit and spin
     Within.
See the grey line of the dim religious sisters.
They will escape the blank unlighted spaces
   Where a love that once lived has died:
But they will never walk in the singing places
   With side pressed to a lover's side.
   Behold, the unimagined pain,
   By which their Mary bore
   Jesus to this life's shore,
     They disdain.
   This done in Thy name
     Almighty God,
     Is it Thy gain?
     Renunciation,
   Poor Sisters? What is it but shame
     And Desolation?

Petronius Arbiter; translation

Ah strand that I love more than life! Ah sea,
    Thou happy sea,
Lapping so oft the shores of my own land!
    Where once (ay me
The beauty of those country days) I'ld be,
    Wooing the Naiads, one at either hand.
Here in this bay, wave-washed seaweed will swing;
    Nearby, the spring
Spreads to a pool. Safe, silent refuge here
    For wantoning,
Here I have Lived! No chance, no fortune-sting
Shall dull the charm of memories so dear.

My soul, my brother's soul, and God's

O heart, enduring heart!
  When ashen pain
Wrings you, and seems it will not cease
  Ever again:
  What is the art,
Poor, shuddering, enduring heart,
  That brings release?
  And heart replies,
'Do I endure alone? Is all pain mine?
  Look in the eyes
Of other men, find there your anodyne,
  Look, if you dare,
  At Holiness
In the deep eyes of your almighty God,
  And marvel there
To see the pain of all the world
  Merge into loveliness.'
  Heart, we will try,
    You and I.

Crazy Head

So, you have laid your crazy head
    for the last time to rest
on the silk-rustling gently stirring dearness
    of her breast:
Boy, for you she is dead.
    There is no magic art
will conjure beneath your hand
    the sweet uneasy throbbing
        of her heart:
Boy, do you understand?
You will not kiss those eyes of hers again,
    those little feet,
Your words, half speech half sobbing,
    stumbling to meet
the gay unpitying air –
While there still faintly lingers
the sweep of farewell fingers
    in your hair
    and your lips hear the note
    of the blood's surge and drain
        in her throat –
These words, half speech half sobbing,
    were the last.
Boy, do you stand aghast?

'That Virginity is a Virtue?' (John Donne)

Do you still think, charming virgin,
How he kissed you in the street ?
Do your heartbeats still come surging . . .
Most disturbing, rather sweet ?
Do you ponder how you smacked him –
Gently – pretty lips set firm ?
Did you know it would attract him
More, although it made him squirm ?
Was it a surprise, when passion
Burst its gates, and you were kissed
In uncompromising fashion ? –
Was it easy to resist ?
No! Those eyes could not be giving
Windows to a heart of ice;
Cold they are, but they are living.
Had he kissed again . . . once . . . twice ? . . .

    .   .   .   .   .

Curious poet, cease from prying
Into lands beyond your song.
Leave her maiden secrets lying
In her breast, where they belong,
And thank God that there still are Maids among us,
When many a flint-heart, non-professing whore –
– 'Advanced Young Woman' – filthy social fungus –
Takes what a man has and then asks for more.

No Kismet

In the dark forests of Africa
  Where the world still is young,
Her cold eyes unlidded, a silent pythoness
    Swings lazily, hung
Gorged from a branch, while the fat and rotten creeper
  Shuts out the steaming air
And strangles life from that other majestic sleeper
    The great Tree standing there.
      In the dark forests of Africa
      Life lives by strife,
      New breath by death.

In the humming hives of America
  Where men are always young,
  You will find them briskly working
    For invisible dollars
    Ceaselessly, without shirking:
They sweat, and are forced to remove their collars.
  In the humming hives of America
    Great hymns are sung
  To progress, in discordant Anglo-Saxon,
  To the strains of the klaxon.

Behind the great encircling wall of China
  Where men were wise before the world was old,
  Steel-covered trains are slinking
To safety, laden with much precious treasure
  And jewel-encrusted gold,
Turned by skilled fingers while life still held leisure.
  For now the Dragon's head is sinking
Before the Orient sun's fresh gas-filled beams.

  He rises on a land which, in an hour,
  Sees thirty weeping yellow babies born.
  O land of earthquakes and the lotus-flower,
    Control your spawn.

In the Red Square there lies a man in pickle
  – Ichabod, Ichabod –
Sleeping beneath the Hammer and the Sickle
Of the land where an automatic earth
  Is struggling to be born
With shiny, new, electric aids to birth;
  The land which bows
Its head beneath oil drips from a machine –
  Crude baptism; and in the cold grey dawn
Full breasted women milk themselves, not cows.
        I wonder what Lenin
    Thinks, lying there upon the Square he trod
      As man, now decorates as God.

But England! There, they tell me, grass is green
And gardens flower, and beauty may be seen.
Come proudly, English men and women, come,
        Regard this slum.

    Where next, my weary soul? Is it retreat?
    For now, I think, only retreat is sweet.
    And so I stand alone by a sighing sea;
        Inland the mist
    Rises about a dream-embowered earth.
    It is so quiet, and I am kissed
    By solitude, and think of death and birth
        Remotely . . .
                    When suddenly
    Out of the East, with clanging wings
        Beating as one
    Come the wild swans, a swift and living arrow
        Moving upon the sky
    Straight for the red heart of the western sun.
        Within my heart there is a stirring,
        Peace is fled, and vision sings,
    Hearing afar off the prophetic whirring
        Of those mighty things,

Seeing them black on heaven's barred scarlet harrow.

    God, God, that glorious flight
        Straightway has stayed
My fainting soul, for now I know
    Surely that life is strife
For you, and my own death
As nothing in the ever living breath
            of Life.
O distant arrow, while you are in my sight
    I shall not be afraid.

He's kissed me once

He's kissed me once and left me
  With tears in my eyes.
O God, my love has left me:
  He foolish, I so wise.

I would have loved him, given
  All love that I possessed
To him; and he has riven
The heart within my breast.

The breast he should have wept on
  When he was tired and weak,
And, baby like, have slept on
  With his hair against my cheek.

In Fear of War

Is it because I am afraid to die
That I fear war ? No, my soul, you and I,
In that great moment when the stars stand still
And we peer from the crest of the unknown hill
To look at Death – we shall not hide our eyes
I think, or wake the Angels with our cries.

Sometimes Death comes to Age as gentle sleep
   With never any more awaking.
   This have I beheld
   And cannot weep
For long, at such a sweet forsaking
Of a trust well and truly held.

And there is quick, black-hooded Death
Swooping upon the company of the brave,
Men who flaunt the flame of our life gallantly
In the implacable eyes of rocks, air, streams:
   And, in a breath,
Death has them and they lie there: no word: no grave.
But their memorial is carven in our dreams.

In war not God, but man will do the killing;
   And, for he is but mortal,
Perhaps our death will lack its right fulfilling,
   And we from the red portal
Come limping back, deformed and eyeless trunks,
   To finish life mad, hideous
   (Bungled by the slaughterhouse)
And shunned by women as wild things shun skunks.

If it is base to fear such death in life,
Then I am base. But surely, Lord, *your* knife
   Need not strike twice
     in sacrifice:
War is not your work, but a degradation,
Forfeiture of our true life's true ending.
   For when You kill,
   O God, it goes not ill
With men: for then they see Your glory, rending
   Their mortal comprehension: Revelation.

The Graces

The Graces did not shirk,
    they were not shoddy;
it is their perfect work,
        your body.
With tender, lavish art
    each limb they wrought;
        intently sought
    each loveliness
    that formerly apart
    had dwelt, to serve
    and play its part;
    until each curve
of throat and thigh and breast
    was brought
    to sinuous rest.
    That smiling mouth,
    soft as the south,
    ah, that is Beauty.
God, God, I cannot miss
this warmth, this glorious duty.
        Come, kiss.

Serpentinia

How pleasant to sit in the park
Before it is totally dark
And watch the young pairs
Hold hands on the grass
While municipal chairs
Cool the middle class arse.

Into our kiss

Into our kiss
   is spilled
all that can never die.
Time has been stilled,
Space passes by
Unseen;
Old Death himself is killed
While you and I,
linger upon our kiss.

City in the West

Behind the sunset's crimson strife,
Invisible, there lies a place
I love. Look in the glass of life,
Remembrance, westward turn your face.
Now, if I shut my weary eyes,
The woods and hills before me swell;
The towered churches stately rise,
To sound the chimes I know so well.
Far, far below – the River;
I tread the steep streets again;
Once more I hear the shiver
Of leaves in whispering rain.
I see the ships go sliding in
To lie at the city's heart,
And hear the market's hum begin –
Dreams, dreams.
              I'm far apart
From that dear, recollected Spring,
With gentle sky and primrose pale,
Where in the dusk my heart would sing
To hear the singing nightingale;
And in the morning sang anew,
As blackbirds, in the almond tree
Cried up the sun into the blue,
While I looked out, to see
The early smoke curl up, with sweet
Embraces for the expectant sky:
Then at the wind's attack, retreat
And vanish with a sigh.
Now, still, those hours are with me, deep
Within; and if I cannot rest,
They bring me to the gates of sleep,
Till I am quite possessed,
  And drowsing, muse upon the beauty
    That is in the West . . .
  Possessed . . . . possessed.

       .   .   .   .   .

So, when I see the setting sun,
  My memory flies behind it.
If men know joy when life is done,
  It's there that I shall find it.

All Visible Things

I have known the gladness of all visible things,
         For I have seen
On the vast azure circle, pinioned wings
         Of birds careen
Then dip, and sink down to the waiting world.
I have watched the young white morning hurl'd
Over the mountain from the arms of night,
         And the moon's pale light
Slanted along the towers by the water.
From wood and secret stream earth's music rises,
         Guide of my rapt hearing
Beyond all thought, amid inspired surmizes
         Twisting and veering –
Voice of beauty's disembodied daughter.
Touching of silken flesh by eager fingers,
Whispered surrender, momentary peace;
– I have had these; – a laughing memory lingers
         Until the end of life's unease.
I remember the scents of home; in recollection
         I see the roofs against the evening sky
And the low windows looking across the lawn;
         I hear the swifts, suddenly crying, high
above the room where those I love were born.
I thought I was safe in the habit of affection.
         I forgot
The last lonely signpost of decision,
With pointing fingers of duty and desire;
The cruel clearness of the self's true vision
         – No urn, no lot –
Only the choice of water or of fire.

Then in that moment to the soul I'll turn,
To the small chapel of the soul,
Lit with pale candles that unwinking burn.
         There I will turn
And watch the tide of things towards me roll.
In silence that is quieter than a wraith

I'll stand.
At my right hand
And at my left, the candles of my faith
Mutely blazing.
Then, having stood a little while
Alone, gazing
Into the eyes of distance, mile on mile,
I shall go back.
I shall go back, back to my life's abode
And once again
Pursue my lonely road
Of pleasure, and of pain.

No War

There is no war within me now,
Your mouth is on my mouth,
Your breast is smooth beneath my hand,
Your hand upon my brow
Is smooth: we are in lovers land,
My mouth upon your mouth

Oh, if your soul was in your breast
Beneath my hand, perhaps at last
I need no longer plough the sand
So deep in search of rest
Perhaps at last, my wanderings past,
I should begin to understand.

In the square below

In the square below, the final tune
        of the restaurant band, having split the night
        allowed the moon to re-unite
with sky and silence. The single sheet
        was hot upon him and he rolled
over, living again the six-days old
joy of adultery. Impossible to greet
        spontaneous union such as this
        for sin since it washed away all tears
        all sorrow, regret, leaving only the gold
                glory
        of the limbs
        groaning together in hymns
                of lamentation
        that only the gods
                had heard.
Sweet, sweet sweet
it had been and must be for many dawns
                again.

        'When will she be home,
the party must be over soon
        she said she would not stay long.'
                And then
        the sound of key in lock
        a smothered voice bidding goodnight,
        a banging door, and silence.

'She said she would come to say goodnight,
        I'll wait
to feel her sweet presence bending above me
        and pull it down
        to whisper in her ear
the words she cannot wait to hear.'
        Ten minutes and still silence.

He rose from bed and knotting the towel

walked down the silent corridor
to where her bedroom door stood open.
        The lights were on
the curtains quite undrawn
        and on the bed she lay, all lover,
the glorious mane of chestnut hair
        spreading an aureole
        on the white cover.

The peerless breasts,
        the navel he had kissed last night
        shone in the light
        and on the floor
were scatterd clothes;
        between the spread legs
        mons veneris gleamed tawny
        against the black stockings that were all she wore.
        She was dead drunk.

Little Mother

Little Mother, Holy Russia,
    Kiev, Moscow, Novgorod,
When did you lift your eyes to God?
Was it on the march to Prussia,
    Trampling on the crooked cross
That you heard the still small voice
    Or was the choice
    Made at the bloody fosse
On Dniester, Dnieper, quiet Don
    And Volga? When did the voice
Return, that seemed for ever gone?
Only the pealing of the bells
Replies, as Holy Russia spells
    The rediscovered tale
            Of God,
Of Father, Son and Holy Grail
In Kiev, Moscow, Novgorod.

Berlin 1945

The year is at its fall. Stilly the trees await
The hour of nakedness, resigned and dumb.
    Only the secret wind, the Messenger
        Sounds the approaching drum
of doom upon the dry leaves' brittle hides.
        He is come,
In this sad season, not for the leaves only.
        He is the Harbinger
For some who walk and talk today in the gate,
Hands hanging slack or fingering skinny sides.
        They wait
Staring, sometimes smiling, but always staring
    At something I do not see.
        I only know
That when the leaves are gone, they too will go
Into oblivion. They seem content.
For them a woman's breast, a man's warm kiss
        Are nothing to a crust.
        They scan the dust
For food, and finding none, return. The bell
In the bombed steeple sounding, is a dirge
Calling their bodies to forgetfulness
        Desired so long,
        And on their ears the song
Of gentle Mary and the saints above
        Telling the tale of love,
That wintry birthday of the little Jesus,
        Falls unattended.
    Stilly the people stare, and smile
Their smiles, resigned and dumb, bereft of mirth.
        Those dulled eyes surely see
        Something that mine do not;
        They see, when Autumn's ended,
        Under each naked tree
        For each his final plot,
Six frozen feet of European earth.

Colonel Dragoslav Pavlovich
of the Royal Jugoslav Army in the
Fatherland, 1941 – ?

Comrade, I do not know today
Whether you are alive or dead,
Nor whether, hunted still, you stray,
A price upon your head.

If you are dead, I wish for you
A soldier's, not a traitor's grave;
If living, may you still be true
To that which you risked death to save.

There was no middle course, I think,
Before our bloodshot eyes
In those days; it was swim or sink,
Plain hell or paradise.

Peace blurs the choice for me. But, Friend,
For you 'tis clear to see,
If you still live, there's but one end,
To die, or to be free.

Is there no room to love

Is there no world to love
    but this round world,
no life to live
    but this life ?
Is to be only to be at strife,
    take all and nothing give;
and is Oblivion hurled
    at last, from the great Void above ?
Is little brother mouse redeem'd
    that screams once, and is still
        between the teeth of brother ferret
            pouncing for the kill ?
And brother ferret, what of him
    with blood upon his jaws ?
At the last end will his proud spirit
    glide through the azure doors
        (in winter-white, absolv'd, redeem'd)
            and there stand still
Gazing clear-eyed upon the Seraphim ?

Only the sunset and the dawn reply,
    only the dew falling,
only the grey moon riding high
    and on the shore curlews calling.

Stalin

Josip!
Josip Vissarionovich!
  Can you hear Me?
  It is I, Jesus.
You are dying, Josip,
  You are almost dead;
The sleep is on you which
  You nightly dread,
The sleep without dreams, without waking, Josip,
  Which brings you near Me.

  Josip!
Can you still see
The gaunt Tiflis Seminary and the fat priests
  Whose teaching bred your unbelief
    In Me,
Who took My name, but lived as beasts
  And made of you a thief?
Yes, they were sinful men, Josip,
  Sinful as you, my dear;
They too fell asleep –
  And now are here
    With Me.

Do you remember the life you used to live
    Little Josip,
  At Goriy on the mountain,
Before you forgot how to forgive?
    Weep,
Weep, little brother,
  Wash in the fountain
Of tears, before you fall asleep.

  Your Mother,
    Josip,
Do you remember how she used to weep
    For you?

She fell asleep, and she too
        Is here with Me.

Do you recall the gentle pointed face
        Of Alliluieva, Josip,
            The grace
Of her touch, her silly fears,
    And her last dry soundless tears ?
            She fell asleep
And came to Me.

        Yes, Josip,
They are all here with Me.
    So now, you see,
It is time for you to kneel
    Weeping as I once wept
        Beneath the olive tree.
    For, after all, Josip,
You are a man as once I too was Man
    So if you can kneel and weep
        And spill your sin,
    You can go back to bed,
        To sleep,
    Quietly, without dread,
        Until you are dead
Beneath the domes of the secret, silent Kremlin.

To Youth on my 47th Birthday

Seven and forty bells have sounded
Since I whimpered first.
I'm tacking on, I'm not quite grounded,
None of my seams has burst.

As long as sun and moon and star
Are visible to my eye,
I'm hovering still not far from par,
It's not yet time to die.

What lesson do I draw from time
Spent in this vale of tears?
How can I teach the young (in rhyme)
The sum of hopes and fears?

It is that nose to ground is dog,
Which ends in rabbit hole,
While head in air is bloody fog
And sends you up the pole.

So look your height and one inch more,
But never give a yard.
You may get rich, you won't be poor;
You *might* become a Card.

Lines to a Dog in Space

Far off, the world can hear
  A heartbeat ticking.
Limonchik, from your sphere
  As you sit licking
The harness in your cabined emptiness
  Hammocked from Pole to Plough,
Can you know the thoughts that press
  Upon you from below?

At the manger, beneath the Christmas storm,
  The quiet ox and the ass, munching the corn,
Were chosen they say to keep our Saviour warm
  The night that He was born.
Now in the man-made orbit, alone, cold but alive
  Limonchik spins, living a novel death
Alone with the infinite, alone with the final dive

  That ends with the end of breath.
Limonchik, will you know
  Something that you can never tell?
In the last moment, when you go
  After your fashion

To render up your life, and the echoing bell
  Tolls for you, will God's compassion
Redeem not only you but us as well?

Scottish Geography

Yon Ayr's sae dark wi' Rhumm and Eigg
    Ah Canna see the Skye,
Ah maun a Wick and licht to Beag
    If Ah'm tae Tigh ma Tigh.

The Sound o' Sleat rings in ma ear
    Altho the sun is bakin';
Ma Tongue is Squrr'd wi Hoy, Ah hear
    A whine in ma Kyleakin.

Iona mon that aims to be
    A mon should drink but Tay;
But och! it's Muck! What wad tae me
    Ma Little Colonsay?

When Eilean plays her wee Tyndrum
    Wi' Glasnachardoch sticks
Ma kelpie says the time has come
    Tae kick against the pricks.

Ma Callender's nae bluidy guid
    Ma Gigha counter's buist.
Ah guess, while Ah'm still in the muid
    Ah'll parachute on Uist.

Winterscape

All still.
Blue the sky, black branches ptarmigan white the snow,
            this perfection
(no wind
it is as though Adam and Eve, forgive them,
            had never sinned)
            breeds reflection.

            Why
should this unearned ocular beauty
(they toil not neither do they spin)
bayonet the guts of man, sad slave of duty
            and make him cry ?

            He is old,
            cold;
but not so cold that he cannot howl Oh
give me back the lost Mesopotamian completeness
black hair, blue veins, white flesh
            of innocent Eve asleep
with Adam's earliest tears, all salt, all fresh
            Scattered upon her sweetness
            because he loves her so.

Windward of the pale trail of aerobatics
            tracing the white sign of infinity distantly
above, in a sum of final mathematics
            to show that nought is nought
            and nought am I,
            there stand the trees –
black, delicate, formal, slightly Japanese.

They stand, line upon line of grenadiers deader than death
            and the end seems at hand
until against the blue perpetual sand
            that is the air, I see my breath.

Essex Evening

Here I stand, and round me the scented limes
  Secretly leaning one to another, whisper,
Nodding against the dark light of the dying sky,
  They whisper
Fearfully, trying to probe the secret of the times, and I,
  Standing beneath them, hear.
  That is, I hear
Until the whispering silence which is the conversation
                          of the limes
Concerning the coming death of our uncertain times
  Is split –
Split by the scream of the jet-borne sky's defender,
                          wings of death,
  Driven by the men of fear.
They are brave. They are brave;
They will die, the first perhaps of the lemmings who
                          are crowding to death.
  Surely the leading lemming is bravest, the one
                          whose breath
    Is dowsed first by the sea ?
    But he is not alive.
Nor are the others, the less brave ones who follow
                          his gallant dive.
    They are all dead. And he
led them, holding the hand of his bride
    Suicide.
This is the knowledge that shivers in the leaves of the limes
    (Who know that they too will die)
As they whisper to one another about the uncertain times
    Against the eternal sky.

The People

Cry of the People to the Rulers

We do not think we want to know
The road you may tell us to go
We don't trust Vicars, but we bray
When someone tries to say us nay.

Cry of the Rulers to the People

The cross we carry is to know
That every Yes leads to a No.
The sun shines and we cut your hay
Knowing that on a rainy day
It will be spoilt, and then that you
Will say that we have missed our cue.
It is not funny. Please don't laugh.
It's hell to be a golden calf.

Voice of the Spirit of Irony

To want all this and heaven too
Is something I have learnt to rue.
The day the beaver meets the skunk
And runs for it, we'll all be sunk.

Northern Parting

The snow is falling
and as the silent northern people know
   the snow
is love. Its quiet kisses, white, fluttering
   melt on the lips as we stand
   hand upon darling hand
   beneath the stuttering
yellow light of the station lamp.

The stamp of the porter's feet
   heralding the train
is unbearable. The sweet
impression of mouth on mouth
   melting the snow, uttering
   the unutterable,
is burned away by the pain
   of parting, when from the south
   the crazy diesel hooters blare
     twice
   and the love-locked pair
     start apart
   shivered by the ice,
   by the cold voice of the ice
saying depart, depart.

The hissing rectilinear bright
   engine surges throbbing
   into our desperate sight
and with its sound drowns out the sobbing
   death of farewell as body from curved body
   slides to the arms of the protecting night.

You of the sun can live and love and pray
and suffer, and nearly die, all through the red hot day.
   But you forgot too soon.
We, facing the cold astringent moon,
   left with the virgin kiss of snow

beneath the white eternal crackling stars
self-frozen into the winterset
    cannot forget,
because we think we know.

John F. Kennedy

For the hard flat voice,
For the hair growing low across the brow,
For the lean figure stooping awkwardly
    forward in the rocking-chair
The funeral steeples drum.

This was a young man, and as you now can see,
One
Who, whether the Gods loved him or not,
Had to die young.

Some
(As the funeral steeples drum)
Are weeping and others wagging a sage head.

But the bronze bells, hung
In the funeral steeples speak
For the rest, who seek
In silence a reconciliation
For this young man dead.

There is no explanation,
Only a certain majesty
Of unexpected death.
And the sad breath
Of the waiting peoples floats
Up to the sky, to the muffled funeral steeples
Where the bells drum.

The Voice

It is the Voice
    calling.
Calling to us, to you, to me
   the voice of choice
     asking
   me and you and us
     to choose.

'Who do you want to be,
     you
   who sit basking
    under a setting sun?
Not knowing how to end
   what was begun
by others beneath a waxing moon?
    How soon
will you learn the art
    that to lose
    is finding,
how far must you go to know
   the precision of decision?'

There is sleep and there is rest
   and they are not the same;
the closed eyes do not mean the quiet heart.
   No. There is rest
only for those who kiss the breast
   of her they dare not name –
    of choice.

The Distant Horns

The distant horns
of the quiet evening sound
  beyond the trees.
Down to the dew-damp ground
  on bended knees
  the cattle settle
brown eyed, contemplative,
    ruminative,
surveying the few, the future morns
  before they go to die.

But the grass on which they lie
  and pastured over, lowing,
    will still be growing
  long after you and I,
    living, loving, crying
  and, in the end, dying
are set in charity beneath the
            churchyard mound.

P. J. G.

Oh, my friend, you have gone
     and we had not met
   For too, too long.
                    The gong was set
     and sounded for you upon
          the instant, the final road
opened, the Trumpets at the far side blaring
   for you, and I not knowing,
      not alas, alas, not enough caring
                    how you were faring.
Oh, the guilt, the loss of love in sowing
   the harvest of sloth, the bearing
of the burden of not enough caring
   for the burdens you bore, swearing
                    as only you could swear
                       blistering the gods,
                       the nameless sods,
     in the deep knowledge of the one God, the only
                    true succour of the lonely,
   who look in the eyes of Truth.
Oh, Ruth, Ruth, Ruth,
     lonely amid the alien corn,
   perhaps in the new perennial fields
                    you may meet.
                    Greet, oh greet
     him for me and let him know
        that the awkward love he lived
                    lives here below.

Aberfan

Sing loud for the dead children,
    Sing if it chokes your throat,
        Sing it by rote
Until it chokes you, blinds your eye;
    Sing the message that does not die.

Sing for the teachers' heart
    That put his arms about the five
        Who stayed alive
One minute more, a little part
    Of the dying breath.
Sing for the death

    That is no death,
Sing for the short living
    That was golden,
Sing for the giving
    That made us all beholden.
    Sing,
For nothing else there is, man, sing.

The Growmore and the Cheeseparer
(Reflections on economic growth with apologies to
Lewis Carrol)

when i saw you and you saw me
we strove with all our might
to mac the figures seem to be
each what we thought was right;
and this although their maudling was
obscured from human sight.

for you the graph curves bulkily
denoted greenwood growth
while i opined they sternly led
towards empowelled sloth.
(both were at odds, because the gods
knew there was some of both).

we strolled along the serpentine,
whence all but we had fled,
and glancing round the lonely scene
you tossed an angry head.
'the sandmen all have left their posts –
a damn disgrace' you said.

'take all this sand,' you roared at me,
    it's marginal, that's clear.
balogh control could shift the lot
in less than half a year.
a billion tons, to coq sur mer,
so that in england, here,

the index of production rose
point six of one percent.
but no! the carpenter has ruled
that sand must not be sent
across the sea. exchange control
says it was never meant.'

you spat, bejewkes, upon the beach
and fondled your computer
while i spoke of the food i'd eat
if i could go and tutor
a young boussac, or get a job
in gutehoffnungshütte.

you shook your gaitskellaqueous locks,
'i give you up' you said,
'up to the economic hocks
in grimondited sin.
you never will pull up your socks –
let's see the new year in.'

we went to the macdougall arms
where, in kalmeadored light,
stood seven neds and seven nics
remarpling on the right
projection for the homeward course
when marginally tight.

the japanese economy
had nothing on the bill
for growth. at compound twelve percent
the ever-shonfil'd till
surpassed all plans macplanners could
have dreamed it would macfil.

'you see!' you cried in ecstacy
'you cannot say me nay!'
and as you spoke, the nics and neds
politely stole away;
while we (once more) were left alone
with ninety pounds to pay.

Penobscot Bay, Maine

Not yet the wind throbbing
  through the bare boughs
    nor the snow
  drifting against the house.
Only a seal, rolling and bobbing
    across the bay
and a cormorant, etched black
  on the liquid gold of it.
Later, when we are far away,
    eyes ears memory
  can we keep hold of it,
freeze in the crystal of the mind
  the shape of the white house on
    the farther island
and the porcupine quills of the firs
    upon the nearer ?
Shall we remember how in the windless air
    the water purrs
on the headland's green grey snout
    or the wonder that behind
the last blue outposts of America
    swam the Atlantic,
  for us the wrong way round ?
    Can we preserve the sound
of the distant stag belling;
    and in the telling
will recollection in the end put out
  the flame of the solitary maple
    ablaze before its time ?
  The shadows are on the tower
where the rangers watch for fire;
  now as the stars grow clearer
    it is time to turn for home.
But here in this evening hour
  with silence skyward bound,
the feet of one English stranger
    stood on enchanted ground.

A Young Wife, dying

Darling, I do not want to die twice.
         In the art
of love your heart and my heart
      have throbbed together
         and whether
      with another's heart
         the throbbing and the sobbing
would be the same I cannot tell.

         For mice
perhaps it is different, I do not know;
            but to go
      at the end with someone else's heart
         when Death us shall part –
      it frightens me, I do not know.

Perhaps I am wrong, but to give eyes
            seems good,
a kidney too, eyes just after death alive
            is lively, good.
But the heart, darling, this is the end
         and the beginning,
without it is neither shrift nor sinning.

Darling, I do not know.
         But it is so
that when we part
      I wish my heart
         to die with me.

And so darling
      give all of me that there is to give
            except my heart.
For since it is my heart that's dying
         it would be lying
      to live with you again
            (all the glory all the pain)
as an I that was not me
      and I would rather go.

Oh, darling, do you see ?

Flowers

Small children of the Holy Ghost
    I learned to know you late;
my eyes were on the heavenly host
    and man's eternal fate.
But when with loss of innocence
    I found what hate could be
and walked head down in sin and sense,
    then I began to see
gypsophila, love-in-a-mist
    speedwell and pimpernel,
alike in this that dawn had kissed
    them all, and wished them well.

The Old Lady

1694 – 1921 – 1971

To the small boy in nineteen twenty one
    stuck in a traffic block
(then as now, it differs but it does not change)
    the eyeless wall of Soane spelt mystery.
      Liverpool Street the objective, the Exchange
        a hazard on the right, the dung
      from the drays in the gutters steaming,
      and the winter rain streaming
      down on that shuffle of history
        the Bank.

Two small words of history, mystery
    solidity improbability
a legend a fact a tradition a mission
    a hate and a fear
      a question a bastion,
  but now to an older man
    a reality.

At nights in Westminster they shout
    'Who goes home ?'
and the lights go out.
    It is only a break
    in the continuity
which leads to Elizabeth from Kings for good or ill;
  this is a lyric in the stuff of the nation.

But away from the dome
    of Paul's Church and Bow Bells,
    stretched on a foundation
      laid by ancient Rome
    the Old Lady also sleeps.

Younger than Parliament in her own existence
    she keeps

her own persistence,
       waking or sleeping
             her own sort of perpetuity.
Perhaps, as she looks at this or that Wren steeple
       she holds in a certain sense
             the conscience of the People.
And for one ageing servant she spells a kind of home.

Lamentl in Esperantl de R. Van Winkl

Schstinkl schstinkl deutsche mark
   up among the nebel.
Quietl poundl's gone to groundl
   'don't disturb' on label.
Pierrot franc'll stay in bancl
   (au clair de la lune).
Lira Carlisay non troppo,
   neither late nor sooner.
Schwitzer frank she like a tank –
   'ow the 'ell you Stopp'er?
Guilder milder but not much –
Schilling – what a whopper!
Belge francl pretty tranq'l,
   not prepared go dutch.
Rouble? Trouble? Wobble? Gobble?
Nyet. – Ivan'll carry.
Dollar? Holler? Thole the Collar?
Mm . . . . Uncle Sam will tarry.

★   ★   ★

All world people under steeple
   weepl – work for money
asking only eatl drinkl –
   breadl milk; no honey.

I sometimes curse
     my stumbling verse
because I *have* to write it.
     But then reflect,
why not perfect ?
No critic's there to smite it.

Northumbria

In this mysterious northern region
      where the Ninth Legion
fought, roistered, defended
      and in the end
            vanished
I am at rest.

Not banished
      but renewed
            by the lovely duty
      of breathing, seeing, listening
            and being.

No fences to be mended
      here; the beauty
of the river's distant bend
      and Cheviots far blue
            viewed
in the precious evening light
      recall anew
invisible gull – haunted Lindisfarne
      grey, glistening and blest.

It is the quiet of the times that lie here
      which makes the diet of peace.
Perhaps they will let me die here
      out of mind and sight;
with them, perhaps, I shall lie here
      in the lost sleep of ease.

Storm

The shaft of gold effulgence
    pours by divine indulgence
        an unimagin'd jewel
        between the breasts
        of the attending hill.
          All rests
      all ceases, all is still.
  Ambition passion pain, all pleasure
    all of them in their little measure
            wait
        upon the wonder
        of the sudden, cruel
    dreadfully open'd gate
          of thunder.

Too little Love

To love enough is not enough.
 The pain which passes pain
  is the knowing
 that I have not loved too much.
This is the reaping of the sowing
 of the middle doctrine that enough is enough,
  which is in turn the stuff
  of much private weeping
   on many a brave face.
 The crutch that gets one from shins to upright,
  into the light
   is love –
not enough, but too much, too much.
This, I suppose, must be the final gain
 that puts You, waking or sleeping
  into grace.

If it comes to the point

If it comes to the point
    we all know how to die
each to our measure, stiff upper lip,
    gibbering about lost treasure
    saying I told you so
        simply petrified
    or marching wide-eyed
        into eternity.
Does the cruel joint
of the times, which is out,
        not shout
at us that we do not know how to live ?
    It is the city of pity
        that is missing;
        even kissing
is depicted as taking not giving,
    not wonder revivified.
        And why ?
Where along this dreadful road
    was the secret of hope lost,
        the river crossed
        of black despair ?

    I shall tell you.
I, the old soldier of the conventional war
    with men of ground, sea, air
    fighting, but fighting with a chance
        that at the end
not all men women children dogs cats and brussel
        would be dead.   sprouts
    Round the last bend
there would still be someone left
        to go to bed
    and make a child in love
        who in its life

would have a choice
to sorrow or rejoice
in the dark forest or under the angel's wing.

No longer so
as total death is now within our span
and if we sing
we sing to keep our courage up
since human accident
for the first time in the Descent of Man
can end it all.
Perhaps He, in His infinite pity
will give us rope
to save ourselves and sail
once more upon the Main of hope,
with love again descried.
Or shall we drive the last ghastly nail
into that wondrous side ?

Belfast: the Abercorn

If, above the gaunt cenotaph
        of the burnt-out restaurant
Knox, Campion, Calvin, Patrick,
    Cranmer and Ignatius Loyola
        with at their head
Magadalen, and the Holy Ghost, the Comforter
        appeared in the sight of all,
    proclaiming that love was paramount;
        and if all the people there
            whoever they were
            fell to their knees
asking forgiveness for what they had or had not done;
        would the Media report it ?

It is not true

It is not true that all is dead or dying,
    not true that retribution
        is on us all.
Not so long as the rampart clouds are lying
    tumbled above the wall,
      fantastic, proud, immune.

But twenty miles away
    is played another tune
        where day
is turned into half-night
    by the old god pollution
    and at the zenith human sight
        is dimmed
and even our free sky unclearly limn'd.

It is the usual construction.
It rests with Man, poor Man
riven with love, self-pity, self-destruction
    and the mountain – moving faith
that can now make a glowering coal tip
    into a little Eden, and the wraith
of the gardens that would have been
    if the Voice had breathed a little stronger
      unheard, unseen,
      over the gate.

    How much longer
      must we wait ?

63

Roe Deer

Against a backcloth of green field,
        seen
          bounding and dipping,
        a double smear of brown.

  A movement of grace
which brings to the face
those bristles of true poetry that never yield
          to reason.

  Two roe deer
  leaping like light,
like grease slipping
over the wall's grey shield
  down and out of sight
into the shelter of the budding wood,
  so lately sere,
but in the accordant season
  newly bright.

How dear, how right, how good
  to have stood there
        unseen.

The Little House

The little house
    crouched on the crag
  how did it earn the matchless grace
that makes it for man, mouse
    and angel
    perpetual ?
  Some gamekeeper, once, chose.
His eyes must have seen the majestic space
  north west south,
  everything but east
where the land humps up to split the worst wind
  so that those who have sinned
  can kneel at one corner or another
  out of the wind, and pray
  seeing the majestic grace of the space
    'Forgive me my brother
  if I have sinned' and the wind
    blows him back to love.
    It seems he must look not only above
        but widely round.
    For the sound
  of the wind at the corners of the house
    and the birds singing
  in the wood at the beginning
  of the majestic avenues of the gracious space
    around below and above
  tell him to look all ways for the winning
    of the small quiet place
        that is love.

500 copies printed by
Will and Sebastian Carter
at the Rampant Lions Press
Cambridge